What Is a Rock?

by Lisa Harkrader

Table of Contents

Introduction 2
Sedimentary Rocks 4
Igneous Rocks 6
Metamorphic Rocks 10
Conclusion 14
Glossary and Index 16

Introduction

Rocks are made up of minerals. Minerals come from nature. The minerals in rocks have been fused together to form a solid hunk. Rock is a material that can be as big as a mountain. It can also be a pebble small enough to toss in a pond.

Rocks fall into three groups. Each group is made a different way. The three groups are sedimentary, **igneous**, and **metamorphic**.

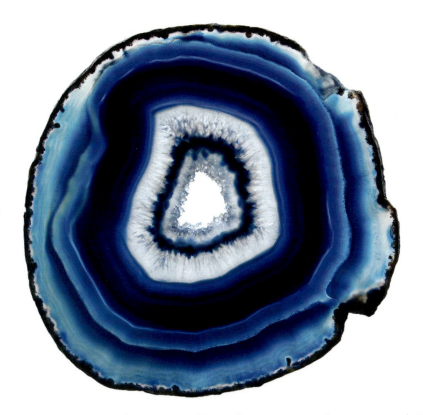

▲ In most rock, it is hard to see the minerals because they are so small. However, in this rock, the minerals appear in different colors.

Sedimentary Rocks

Sedimentary rocks are made up of small bits of sand and dirt, called **sediment**.

Water and wind make bits of rock crumble and wear away. Over the years, this sediment makes layers on the ground. Over millions of years, these layers are pressed together to become sedimentary rock.

▲ Most of the rocks on Earth are sedimentary rocks.

▲ Many pyramids in Egypt were built with limestone.

One kind of sedimentary rock is limestone. It is made up of tiny bits of seashells pressed together under water.

Limestone can be rough or smooth. It usually has a light color. It can be crushed and used to make cement.

Igneous Rocks

Deep in the earth, rock gets so hot that it melts. Melted rock is called magma. As magma cools, it hardens. Rocks made from cooled magma are called igneous rocks.

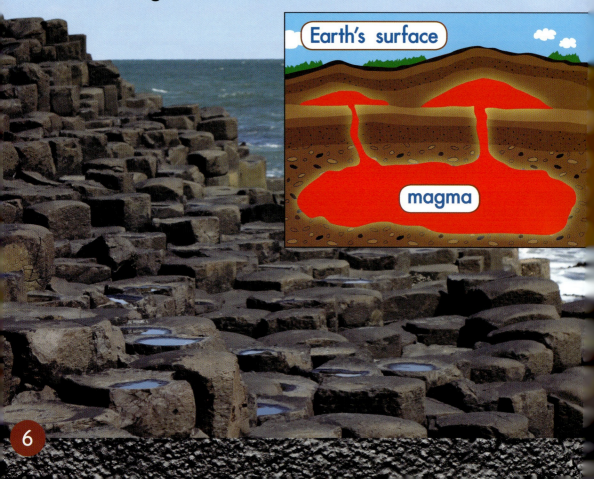

Underground, magma cools very slowly. **Granite** is an igneous rock that is formed underground. The word *granite* means "grainy." It is a very hard rock. We use granite in buildings. It can be polished, or rubbed to make it shine.

The base of the Statue of Liberty is carved from granite. ▶

Sometimes heat and gas build up underground. Then magma pushes through the earth's surface. When magma comes out of the ground, it is called lava.

▲ Lava erupts from volcanoes.

Above ground, the lava cools quickly. It becomes igneous rock that is smooth and glassy.

Another kind of igneous rock is filled with holes. It is called **pumice**. Pumice is made from foamy, gas-filled lava. As the lava cools, the gas bubbles pop, leaving holes in the rock.

▲ This is an igneous rock that looks like black glass.

▲ Some pumice is so light it can float on water.

Metamorphic Rocks

Two forces form metamorphic rock: heat and pressure. These two forces make the rocks change.

This type of rock is very dense. That means the parts are packed tightly together. Many metamorphic rocks have layers of light and dark.

▲ This metamorphic rock came under so much pressure that it folded.

A metamorphic rock is basically a cooked sedimentary or igneous rock. This means all metamorphic rocks begin as another kind of rock. Marble is a kind of metamorphic rock. It comes from the sedimentary rock limestone.

▲ The Taj Mahal, in India, was built of white marble.

Another kind of metamorphic rock is slate. Slate comes from shale, a sedimentary rock made up of clay minerals. Slate can be split into thin sheets.

▲ Slate is used for roof shingles and floor tiles.

Conclusion

Rocks look like they never change. However, rocks are always changing. They build up on Earth's surface. They break down. Around and around it goes, year after year.

Glossary

granite (GRA-nit) a very hard igneous rock often used in buildings; granite is often polished (page 7)

igneous (IG-nee-us) rocks formed when liquid rock cools (page 3)

metamorphic (meh-tuh-MOR-fik) rock that has been changed by heat and pressure (page 3)

pumice (PUH-mis) rock formed from lava that has cooled quickly; pumice has many holes and is lightweight (page 9)

sediment (SEH-dih-ment) small bits of rock, clay, or dirt worn away from the earth's surface (page 4)

Index

granite, 7
igneous rock, 3, 6–7, 9, 12
metamorphic rock, 3, 10–13
minerals, 2–3, 13
pumice, 9
sedimentary rock, 3–5, 12–13